Breaking Eighty

To my great neighbors, Bruce and Becky,

Charles Halsted

poems by

Charles Halsted

Finishing Line Press
Georgetown, Kentucky

Breaking Eighty

For Ann
and for my children and grandchildren

ACKNOWLEDGMENTS

Many of these poems were first published in

Blood and Bourbon: "Bourbon Street Awakening"
Blood and Thunder: "Quality of Life"
Clerestory: "Upside Down"
Contemporary Poetry: "Senior Moments"
Degenerates: "Homeless Shelter"
The Ghazal Page: "Forget-Me-Nots"
Haibun Today: "Breaking Eighty"
Hektoin International: "Redemption," "Letter to Pa"
Killjoy: "Feather River"
Medical Literary Messenger: "Mouth to Mouth"
The Moon: "Navajo Medicine," "Hopi Dancers"
Poetry Now: "Waking Rituals"
Rosette Maleficarum: "The Monster of Darkness"
Siren's Call: "Bombs in the Night"
Sisyphus: "Initiation Night"
Snapdragon: "Bucket of Blood," "Spirits in the Ceiling"
Tule Review: "Evolution Valley"
The Turnip Truck(s): "Grandma's Corpse"
Wood Coin: "In the Footsteps of the Parisian Poet"
Words Apart: "Extenuating Circumstances"
Yolo Crow: "Pacific Daybreak," "Rainbow Ride," "Return of the Magpies"

"Bombs in the Night" was among the Laureates' Choice winners of the 2017 Great
River Shakespeare Festival's Maria W. Faust Sonnet Contest.

Publisher: Leah Maines
Editor: Christen Kincaid
Cover Art: Cindy Davis; http://www.cindydavisphotography.com/
Author Photo: Cindy Davis; http://www.cindydavisphotography.com/
Cover Design: Leah Huete

Printed in the USA on acid-free paper.
Order online: www.finishinglinepress.com
        also available on amazon.com

Author inquiries and mail orders:
Finishing Line Press
P. O. Box 1626
Georgetown, Kentucky 40324
U. S. A.

Table of Contents

The Monster of Darkness

As a child, he was warned not to seek the Googeebocky,
a beast half human, half spider that dwelled in the dark
of the attic closet where the end was inky black.
The door screeched on its hinges, had neither lock nor key.
Whichever child entered no longer would be seen,
swallowed whole with neither trace nor spark
of life, no opportunity to embark
on childhood, of which the monster made a mockery.

As a man, he learned that a cancer had appeared,
the kind that would quickly spread throughout his stark
naked body if not cut out very soon, he was told.
He trusted his surgeon, though frozen stiff with fear,
since he knew he must pass through a tunnel so black
that the monster of darkness could devour him whole.

Bombs in the Night

Tar balls on beaches, blackouts every night
meant battles at sea and German subs near shore.
My English schoolboy pen pal was taken from the sights
of bombers sowing terror on the innocents of war.
The man who pumped gas at the Pegasus sign
was arrested, tried, and convicted, a Nazi spy.
Our fathers were gone, my friend's was killed in France,
while mine, a doctor, was safe behind the lines,
sorting the sick from those too scared to fight.
I dreamed of bombs and fires across the fields,
the creatures of nearby woods in frantic flight,
and invented a ritual to shield me from fear,
to assure my father's return, a secret rite
that endured to prevent the return of bombs in the night.

How to Sip Beer

Big brother and I, sixteen in fifty-three,
with two other guys and a thirty-six Ford, just right,
drove Boston-L.A. in three days. We stopped in D.C.,
where I gazed up in awe at martyred Lincoln by moonlight,
then on through the night in the battle-scarred South
where our Union great-grandpa fought to free the slaves,
arriving next day at the Mississippi's mouth.
At evening we strolled along Bourbon, the street paved
with sin, and entered a strip joint where I was shown
how to sip beer while staring at flesh never seen.
We crossed the southwestern desert nonstop and wind-blown,
the Mojave on razor-thin tires at one-twenty degrees.
Big brother kept me awake my last turn as a pup.
We'd reached California, where I was bound to grow up.

Bourbon Street Awakening

He strolls along Bourbon. It's a warm summer's eve.
Partiers toss trinkets from balconies.
Trumpeters thrust jazz through open doors,
hoping he'll enter to hear them play.

Only sixteen, he's driven nonstop two days
with his older brother and two other guys.
They've stopped for a break, an overnight stay
in this mecca at the Mississippi's mouth.

Halfway along, a barker calls out.
The door's cracked open to a darkened room—
a strip joint. He stops to stare; he's heard
of such places but has never been inside.

Big brother shows how to belly up to the bar,
drink his beer slowly, make it last half an hour.
This is the first drink he's had unshared.
It doesn't matter he's underage—nobody cares.

Up on the bar, she appears fully clothed,
starts to gyrate, undoes buttons and straps.
A background trio grinds out her refrain.
All present fall silent, eyes fixed on her dance.

Her artistry's in her curves and her moves.
When the music stops, she flashes a smile,
scoops clothes from the floor, and disappears.
Beer glass now empty, he's no longer a child.

Evolution Valley

"You can stay overnight at my place," she says,
thirty-five, tight-ass jeans, two shirt buttons undone.

My pack train makes its way along the trail.
Not quite sixteen, I'm the go-to kid from L.A.
It's the end of summer; next week I go home.
Three months on the job, and I've become
the guy who throws hitches on horses' backs,
leads a packhorse train through mountains
thousands of feet high to utopian valleys.
We wind through switchbacks that hug
the mountainside above a roiling river.
One hoof off the trail, the pack train would fall—
all six horses, the dudes, and I would plunge down.

Should I go to her bed in San Francisco
or take my chances with teasing teenage
Circes and Sirens back home in L.A.?

At dusk we arrive at a green valley meadow;
a dark forest surrounds it, a river ripples through,
distant snow-capped peaks glow in the setting sun.
I untie hitches, unload belongings,
hobble the horses to keep them nearby,
make the campfire blaze, prepare canned dinners.
She and the others sleep by the fire.

I make my bed at river's shore,
Contemplate virginity and the stars.

In the Footsteps of the Parisian Poet

Dutifully, he trails high heels clicking
up rickety stairs, treads so worn they could
have been climbed by Baudelaire on nightly
forays a hundred years before, howling
after one or more of his favorite whores.

The room is square, cracked ceiling, paint
peeling, washbasin at the wall, single bed
centered on the floor. His tutor, Piaf-like,
perhaps forty, orders him to drop his trousers
and drawers. With a flick of her tongue, he's
quickly undone. Wet washcloth tossed in the sink,
she remains standing, still fully clothed.

In his best college French he asks: *"Est-ce fini?"*
As she turns away, he exclaims, *"Vous m'avez trompé!"*
Murmurs and laughter of other *putes de la rue
Pigalle* rise through the window cracked open
to the perfumed Parisian twilight.

That evening he hears a French couple
across the room undressing, caressing.
He listens to their rhythmic bedspring song,
stares at the ceiling above his hostel bed.

Forget-Me-Nots

While travelling abroad in his twenty-first year, he vowed to be true
to widening his views. He met a French girl who turned out to be true

to all he desired. For two weeks they discussed Voltaire and Camus
in a small Alpine village far up from view. This brief story is true.

She taught him to tie flowers both yellow and blue, into
garlands for her hair of *ne m'oubliez pas*, forget-me-nots, the true

translation. Yet these days of dalliance wore on, became ever few,
till his vagabond life beckoned him once more to be true

to expanding horizons in strange lands and places, all new, to heed
Shakespeare's advice: "This above all: to thine own self be true."

Grandma's Corpse

Sixteen shroud-covered corpses lay on steel tables, awaiting our first day of medical school. The windows opened to the street and the city graveyard beyond, marked with row upon row of granite headstones. When we pulled back the shroud, formaldehyde wafted up from someone's dead grandma or mum. We drew straws to decide who'd make the first cut. I picked up my scalpel and drew it through the skin of her bloodless chest and abdomen.

We each took a turn extending incisions, digging deep into the framework of her former life's functions. Her bloodless heart, a grapefruit, no longer pumped blood; her lungs, collapsed beach balls, no longer breathed air. We dissected each of twelve cranial nerves, conduits of life senses, their diverse roles learned by mnemonics bequeathed by students long gone. Lifting the veil of abdominal fat revealed her rubbery liver, an energy factory silenced by death, and her kidneys, toy footballs tucked up on each side. Her guts, former channels for food and waste, extended the length of the table she lay on.

Many weeks later, dissection done, all that remained were scraps of muscle and bone. Our corpse had made her final donation, the bedrock of our medical educations. Her remains had earned their rest in the cemetery across the street, after a spell in the hospital crematorium.

Navajo Medicine

Blustering winds foretold a desert storm,
spiraling sand: a dark funnel cloud. Two teenage
boys climbed to the top of sacred Navajo
Mountain, silhouetted by darkening sky.

They arrived at our U.S. Indian Hospital
in the back of a pickup truck: one stone
dead, the other babbling chaos. Lightning
had stricken each through from head to toe.

We did what we could to keep him alive until *hatáli*,
the medicine man, appeared as if an apparition.
His diagnostic Hand Trembling rite revealed
imbalance of his patient's spirits.

The Holy People of Navajo Mountain
considered the climb taboo transgression.
Exorcism of this grave offense required
the consummate Night Way incantation.

Hatáli sang and chanted nine days and nine nights
to restore the boy's ties with the Holy People,
to sustain tribal bonds while cleansing his soul,
to restore harmony to the Navajo Nation.

The Navajo boy walked away, while we *bilagáana*,
white doctors, stood silently by, awe stricken.

Hopi Dancers

Since time out of mind, the Hopi tribe
maintained its customs, dances, beliefs,
then resisted conversions by Catholic priests.

Back in summer of '61, we, the only two whites,
stood quiet in the Oraibi *plaza* with reverent
native villagers, to witness the ritual dances
of men and boys of the Hopi Nation.

For the warm-up dance to disparage the Spanish past,
two Hopi men dressed in black robes as priests of conversion.
Another played Christ with a crown of thorns, ascending
a ladder to Oraibi's roof of heaven. He was turned back
to the plaza by Hopi men at the top, who unzipped
and rained piss on the priests below.

In the rattlesnake pubertal rite, ten Hopi men,
each masked as a different *kachina*, or animal spirit,
encircled a closed wooden trunk. When the lid
was opened, each man reached in to grasp the neck
of a snake, sedated by darkness but ready to writhe.

Dancing in the circle to the sounds of thrumming drums,
each *kachina*-masked man passed his snake to a pubertal
boy, naked but for a loincloth. Each initiate placed the neck
of a snake in his teeth, continued the circular dance. After
ten turns, each snake was returned to the sandy middle.

Four well-chosen brave men dashed in, grabbed two
or three writhing snakes apiece by their necks, and raced
off to the desert in four compass directions. In this
fashion, each messenger snake from the holy ancients
was returned to its home in the Hopi Nation.

Initiation Night

The pager beeps the end of my sleep. It's midnight; I'm the one on call. I quickly rise to make my way through basement tunnels where ancient pipes crisscross the ceilings, scuffs of gurneys mark the walls. Caged faint bulbs light the way, as they have for scores of interns from decades before.

I board the creaking lift to examine the newest patient, an alcoholic with liver failure in full DTs, then walk down the darkened hallway, enter each half-open door. Most of my patients sleep with their disorders; the eyes of the others reveal their fears. A homeless guy with frost-bitten feet seeks to survive the freezing northeastern winter. An aging hooker with acute PID has nowhere else to spend the night. A grizzled old man with pneumonia breathes fast, then shallow, coughs up putrid secretions that tell me his death is near. The remaining sick suffer other diseases, each one requiring my full attention.

The duty nurse, who's twice my age, asks which orders I'd like to change. I write down what seems best for each one's survival through the night. At six A.M., a glimmer of sun shines through the belching factory smoke of our city in aging decay. As the nurse prepares to leave her station, her thanks say I'm now part of the healing profession.

Quality of Life

I slid in the scope past ridges and caves,
along a dark tunnel with purplish seams—
twisting and turning till finally it gave
out to a space where a pebbly lump gleamed.

From the end of the tunnel with purplish seams,
his life would be shortened by bloody ooze
into the space where the pebbly lump gleamed.
I slipped forceps through to give me a clue

from a piece of the lump with its bloody ooze,
which I sent to the lab to find out why he bled.
Cancer was the answer to the pebbly lump clue.
I'd have to tell him now, though the news would be dread.

When he awoke I told why he bled.
"You've saved my life," was his reply.
Although the long-term prognosis was dread,
with surgery, he would not yet die.

To live life to the full was his reply
to the cards he'd been dealt by unwelcome fate.
Though his life might be short, he would not die
till he'd done all he could that remained on his plate.

For six long years he ignored his fate.
He traveled and painted, did all he had planned,
put aside all fears that remained on his plate,
till a spot appeared on a liver scan.

The cancer's return was not part of his plan.
Chemo became his only choice,
with puking and numbing and further scans,
until I had to tell him with quavering voice:

"No more can be done, you've no more choice,"
knowing full well that in weeks he'd be dead.
He rose from his chair and replied with clear voice:
"You gave me six years of life," was all that he said.

Redemption

I'm high on crack and going eighty,
black rainy night, oncoming lights,
back seat guy shouts out "Look out!" too late.
I cannot breathe, my chest's come tight.
Pain cuts my guts, knifes through to my back.
Ambulance screams, tears through the night.
ER docs crowd me, I'm under attack.
Up to the OR, all's black, nothing's right.
My guts are torn, they cut them out.
My fractured back will never be straight.
Condemned from now on to be fed by IV,
from gangbanger to cripple, that's now my fate.
My hospital room's filled with darkness, despair—
death's everywhere, in hallways, in air.
My past's come back, soon I must die,
when an angel as chaplain appears at my side.
She speaks of redemption and sin's retribution:
forgiveness of self is the final solution.
There's a way forward, of that I'm now certain.
I can pray to God, I need no permission.
I did not cheat death, I'm here for a reason.
My body's been broken, but my soul's been restored.
I'm reconnected to forces unseen,
I'm in spirit's realm, I've been redeemed.

Bucket of Blood

He arrived at the ER half dead, stone drunk,
from the Bucket of Blood in Baltimore.
Feet frost-bitten, arms of a skeleton,
shaky hands, tongue red as a beet,
eyeballs yellow as mustard.

Spider-web veins covered his chest;
gurgling noises rippled through his lungs.
Belly swollen, liver like a basketball,
he babbled on with persons unknown.
Blood alcohol high, his outlook was grim.

Up on the ward, he puked up red blood.
Emergency scoping found a burst vein.
Blood pressure was low, pulse fast and weak,
but improved with drug transfusions.
No one who knew him appeared.

Ten days later, he was ready to go—
no longer confused, blood tests improved,
eating well, as good as he would ever be.
His parting words: "Thanks, Doc, come
with me, I'll buy you a drink at the B of B."

Mouth to Mouth

Emerging from the swarming hornet horde,
I tear at seventy over the boundary bridge,
glance down at the dirty brown river, foresee
a straight shot through the traffic to home.

I scan the wetlands on either side.
A flock of crows hovers as one
above a marshland of brush and canals.
A great egret stands still, a white speck on a shore.

There's a cluster of cars on the shoulder.
Caution tells me it's time to slow down.
A big rig has pulled over. The driver
lies flat on his back on the ground.

My professional oath tells me what I must do:
stop at the roadside, preserve life, prevent death.
I say the words that announce my profession.
The crowd retreats to the shoulder's outside edge.

I lean over to look at my patient, a fallen statue,
grossly obese in a sweat-soaked shirt, has a slight drool.
I steel myself for mouth-to-mouth breathing, chest compressing,
releasing, to bring him back to inhale on his own.

I feel deep in his neck for a pulse, find none. His face is gray,
his eyes glazed. "Too late," I announce to the crowd,
"this man is already dead." A wailing ambulance crosses
the center divider, stops to load him aboard, and he's gone.

The great egret flaps up from the marsh, circles overhead.
I return to my car, reenter the freeway, slowly drive home.

Homeless Shelter

The nomadic poor of our town trudge silently through
the gate, check in at our program site for an overnight stay
at one of the churches nearby. The men wear five-day
stubbles, women threadbare sweaters, old clothes.
A volunteer, I serve coffee, observe, provide a listening ear.

An old man with a grease-spattered shirt and wobbly
gait appears burnt out from years of sloshing down booze.
A wandering woman in unwashed clothes grasps
at my sleeve, mutters her woes. A well-dressed young
woman in red beret stares quietly down at the floor.
A shitfaced young guy with slurred speech starts a fight;
we call the town cops who take him away.

A tall black guy with an afro stands still as a statue,
meditating against an inside wall. Two ex-cons
with skull and snake tattoos need bus passes to meet
their paroles. Two outcast young lovers touch hands,
long for better days. A businessman tells us
his wife kicked him out, silently scans the *New York Times*
to show us he's not their kind.

Tomorrow, some will seek work and a place to live, but most
will shuffle the streets until dark, wait for spring's return
to reclaim their old spots by the tracks out of town.

Pacific Daybreak

Dawn rims the mountains across the bay.
Waves roll and crash in eternal show;
bursting foam heralds the newborn day.

Glints on the sea reflect sun's rays.
Waves reach skyward as sea winds blow;
dawn rims the mountains across the bay.

Searching shorebirds skip along the quay.
Waves break like shots on rocks below;
bursting foam heralds the newborn day.

Brightening sun is filtered by spray.
Sea rushes up in ebb and flow;
dawn rims the mountains across the bay.

Pungent odors pervade the air.
When waves recede and tide is low,
seaweed is unveiled by light of day.

Underground creatures thrown into the fray;
life spawns on rocks beneath the foam.
Dawn rims the mountains across the bay;
bursting foam heralds the newborn day.

Rainbow Ride

We rode out on a late winter morning,
a fast trot atop a levee by a farm ditch in our valley
that stretches from Shasta to Tehachapi,
from the Sierra Nevada to western hills,
now greenish gray and ever in our distance.

We tripped along the roadway splashing mud on either side,
his nostrils flared, ears upright with fine-tuned hairs,
wind-tossed mane, his pounding muscles next to mine,
as I, close reined, captured his power with my legs,
crotch, and spine, and the earth called out to us.

We thought we'd find old friends who'd tell
of the coming spring: the great heron in the reeds
of a close-by pond where fish are seen jumping
on warmer days, the red-winged blackbirds
that sit on the phone lines and sing to the wind.

Jackrabbits zigzagged up and down the plain,
just-flushed quails tore across our view,
chirping sparrows wheeled about, and the great heron
rose up, wings flapping, and settled in a distant field.

Dark clouds came down to wash our faces
with Pacific rain, then gave way as sun-washed
green grass foretold the season's change.

Waking Rituals

At first light, the cars below begin to move.
I hear the distant moan of the early dawn freight;
closer in, the gentle coos of the mourning dove.

Still in my cocoon, I roll towards
her sleep-shrouded nakedness,
spoon my bony angles around soft curves.

I'm awake and alive, while with
rhythmic rise and fall of her rib cage
she sleeps on warm and still.

Birds start to call, some shrill, some peeps.
Low washboard stutters of magpies
announce the gathering light of the sun.

Gray turns to gold across fields of wheat,
distant oaks from dark to brilliant greens.
Sunlight bursts through close-in leaves.

I splash cold water on my face,
get the tea water up to a boil.
Scalding heat, oxygen, and tiny leaves

burst magical aromas and tastes
all the way from Ceylon to my brain.
My senses now at their height,

I move into the day.

Return of the Magpies

Two each to a silvery leaf-bare branch,
eight sit quiet in our front yard birch,
heralding the season's change,
sharp yellow bills, white breasts,
wings and tails of green and blue.

Overhead more call out kut-scree,
declaring their space from
caw-cawing crows in hasty retreat
far from our neighborhood trees.
How did they know
they'd find safe haven here?

Why such precision of colors
to bring enchantment to my day?
Is it all in their DNA?
O master molecule of life!
Your helical staircases
uncoiled, an arm's length in each cell,

each helix linking quaternary codes
in sixty-four permutations,
unzipping and doubling as cells divide,
transcribing the codes
for the proteins that signal
all intricate processes of life,

that make yellow bills, white breasts,
dark blue wings, long tails to fly,
all the flight maps in their brains,
their kut-kut scree-scree songs,
their monogamous matings to survive,

while my own DNA creates vision,
finds beauty in this first sign of spring,
as the same quaternary codes
spin spiral staircases in my brain,
transcribe the signals that discover
mystery in DNA, miracles in magpies.

Senior Moments

You cannot place her name, her face
from just last week or long ago, when now
was mixed with hope and not the past.

You do not know if your aching rib
is just a recent but forgotten bruise
or return of the cancer cut out years ago.

You do not know if your heart will last the night,
or stop at three billion beats since you were born
before the start of the Second World War.

But you know that light will appear at half past six,
the freight will rumble at dawn through the fields,
the lilacs bloom purple, the redbuds in pink.

The magpies will call from your backyard trees,
an Eastern aroma will rise from your tea,
and chances are you'll have twenty more years.

How to Catch a Steelhead Trout

It's dark as pitch at boat launch on the river.
The hull rocks as you board, your heart's aquiver.
The dawn's just a sliver of sun in the east.
The early light of October foretells a feast.

The roiling river surface reveals thrashing tails
as salmon shower sperm on the eggs of females.
But the prey you seek lies downstream of the spawn:
the steelhead dance for the eggs begins at dawn.

You must outwit your fish by your cast of fake fly
to fall upstream of where the creature lies.
Its grab sends a jolt up your line—you must jerk
your rod straight back to set your hook.

Your fish will then turn to race down the stream.
To shake itself loose, it will jump and careen.
If you keep the right tension hard on your reel,
excitement will build with each fish move you feel.

When at last your steelhead starts to tire,
you must wind your reel fast if you aspire
to bring the fish to your net and to land by the range
of orange-flamed trees that announce season's change.

Upside Down

Inferno

Upside down in fast-moving current, my death but seconds away:
boulders below, the demons who'd break my bones,
branches above, the harpies who'd end my day.

Eyes fixed on a bank-side bloom, I'd pulled the wrong oar,
while fishing the wide Rogue River alone.
My pontoon boat had flipped when it met the shore.

From deep within came a voice without sound
that broke through my terror, as if in a dream:
"If I can keep my head on straight, I will not drown."

I jerked the cord to inflate my vest when I was far downstream.
Breaking the surface upright, survival became my only aim.
I gained a foothold, breathed deeply in, surveyed the scene.

Purgatorio

Waves crashing on rocks below foretold my death by maiming,
but the river above me flowed calmly as my very own
capsized boat and one oar floated down, my life sustained.

I swallowed my pride to have fished the river alone,
recanted all the audacity left in my soul,
grasped the oar, boarded my boat that was still upside down.

Stroking hard to escape the demon rocks, I paddled my pontoon
across the river with strength till then I'd never known,
and reached a place to turn it upright in a quiet lagoon.

Paradiso

I spied two fishermen in a boat not fifty yards below.
They rowed to me with a second oar, a rescue from my plight,
since the journey to takeout was still a mile-long row.

I drifted downstream hearing songbirds singing, watching ducks alight.
A treetop eagle spied a reckless fish that soon would pay its cost.
Deer bowed their heads to drink while geese soared over in flight.

Making landfall at last, I was met by a fisherman host.
With outstretched hand, he said: "Take this cold beer!"
I'd reached a grace I vowed would never again be lost.

My River Princess

My stuttering line came tight, sure sign that I
had hooked a steelhead trout at early dawn,
cavorting in roiling water, the spawning ground.

I jerked back my rod, set hook through fish lip, lowered
the rod-tip, loosened the line, and watched as it leapt,
careened, somersaulted its way down the stream.

With line held tight, I reeled the fish into my net,
carefully walked it up to the shore now bathed in full sun.
Three feet in length, its belly and sides were coated
with white flecks of sperm. I had hooked a wily
steelhead trout in the very act of sex.

I laid it down upon the ground and went to find the knife
I would use to slice it open and rip out its guts,
after bashing its head with a rock to be sure it was dead.

When I turned back to gaze with pride on my prize, I found
an upright coquette with rosebud nipples and flowing
black hair. I pulled her close to my chest, slid my hand down
her spine, and felt with surprise a slimy green bottom and tail.

With arms outstretched, I lowered her gently back in the stream,
gazed sadly while she glided away as I stood alone on the shore.
Released from my embrace, my river princess swam quickly
back to rejoin the orgy of spawn.

Leda's Choice

Anticipation turns to mounting desire.
She draws its downy neck closer and sighs.
Grasping wings assure it will sire,
when, in wordless dance, she parts her thighs.
While she fulfills her secret assignation,
the cuckold king impatiently awaits,
oblivious, preparing her impregnation
in their rock-bound castle far off in the haze.
The bastard babes look up in complicity;
what meets their gaze will become inheritance.
Their destinies are promiscuity;
endless warring humanity's dance.
From Helen of Troy to weapons of depopulation:
all these the fruit of this strange copulation.

Feather River

While standing in California's Feather River,
casting my fly over rippling waters,
I remembered from family letters that
great-grandfather had mined for gold upstream.

Out from Boston, age twenty-five, he wrote
in letters home to his Ma: "The natives
in the woods nearby are not the noble savages
we've read about in Cooper's tales.

"Dirty blankets are all they wear,
with sticks in long and shaggy hair.
My friends go out to kill them for sport
on Sundays after noontime prayers."

Awaiting the pounce of an eager fish,
I recalled the genocide of native tribes
at the hands of miners and settlers
who lusted for their land and lives.

When I came home with empty hands,
I opened up a tiny box
to gaze at my inheritance:
a golden wedding band inscribed

1855 on one side,
Feather River on the other.

Extenuating Circumstances

Sacramento, California, *2013*
Car runs over black man
in downtown shopping mall.
Driver tells police he deserved it.
"Now that they have Obama,
they think they're just real special."

Phoenix, Arizona, *2012*
Two hundred Mexican-Americans
arrested, jailed in tents at 120 degrees.
Sheriff Joe tells the press:
"So it's O.K. for our soldiers to live in hot tents,
but it's wrong for inmates?"

Haditha, Iraq, *2005*
Children shot in pajamas, father with his Koran,
twenty-four in one family gunned down.
Blood-spattered beds, furniture, walls,
"To teach them a lesson they'll never forget:
all terrorists must die."

My Lai, Vietnam, *1968*
Babies bayoneted, mothers machine-gunned,
terrified children cower behind.
Huts burned down by Zippos to the thatch,
three hundred and more. *"They must be VC,*
all commies must be stopped."

Selma, Alabama, *1965*
Northern white Unitarian minister
joins civil rights march at Pettus Bridge,
dies after blow to head with baseball bat.
Last words he hears: *"You want to know*
what it's like to be a nigger 'round here?"

Bullard's Bar, California, *1855*
My great-grandfather digs for gold,
writes home to his mother in Boston:
"The Indians here are not the noble
savages of Fenimore Cooper; my friends
shoot them on Sunday afternoons."

Spirits in the Ceiling

"Martha! We were pals long before your fame,
how I wish my beaux had been like yours!"

"Hallucinating?" I ask the hospice nurse.
"Is this the last stage of dying?"
"No," she says, "they're her long-lost friends
returned to dance in the ceiling.
She's getting ready to go
to their eternal party
in that space between the stars
and all the molecules of life."

A small cardboard box holds
gray ash and tiny white pieces
of her hundred-year-old bones,
gritty but easy to sift through our fingers.
We mix her remains with the soil
of a brittle young quince with orange buds
far above the blue-green sea and granite shore,
where gulls and breaking spray flash white in the sun,
the never-ceasing to and fro of crashing waves,
the constant refrain of her world.

We water the quince before walking away.

Letter to Pa

I heard our tire chains clacking on slushy
streets, then waited freezing, short legs
dangling, watching you—warm coat
against the cold, your bag in hand—walk
through the opened door, return after
half an hour with a loaf of fresh bread, the way
you were paid in those late depression years.

A few years later, world war raging,
a neighbor's kid crossed the street
to beat me up. His dad was killed in France,
while you were safe behind the lines,
taking care of wounded men. I dreamed
each night of bombs and fires, invented
a secret rite to assure your safe return.

Ten years had passed when you divorced
my Ma and I had you for my own. I felt
my pride and your elation when you described
your research on vitamin B12.
I chose to follow in your career, your footsteps,
as it's said, with twenty more years to train
till I became a medical scientist on my own.

When you died at seventy-eight, I was
forty-seven with thirty years more in my career.
My medical science and skills became
ingrained within my deepest self. When
my career came to its end, I found myself
adrift, yet, always mindful, still your son.

Breaking Eighty

At seventy-eight, I ran up ten granite stairs in a violent East Coast summer rainstorm, tripped, crashed forward head first, and bled profusely from a long gash in my forehead. After a wailing ambulance ride to the nearest ER, a young woman doc stitched me up, my attentive teenage granddaughter at my side. Once seen in the clinic back home, I learned that my head MRI was OK, while cognition tests showed minimal change. I'd entered the realm of the aged.

At seventy-nine on a family climb, I stood on a ledge looking down hundreds of feet through tops of towering pines. I imagined a fall that would break arms and legs on branches, splatter my brains across the forest floor. As I wobbled over walking poles in mounting panic, my elder son grasped my outside arm, asked "Dad, you OK?", and led me past my certain demise.

When I'd turned eighty, my college-aged granddaughter asked, "Grandad, how did you design your experiments?" Enchanted, I led her through the scientific method, second nature in my former career. My grandson, a tireless teenage athlete, chimed in: "Grandad, what was your best time in the two-mile run?" I replied, "Ten minutes, twenty-eight seconds in my last freshman track meet," adding that my alumnus donation requests always begin: "Dear student athlete." Eighty did not seem so old when my grandson replied: "Awesome time, Grandad!"

slanting sun
on golden oak leaves—
crickets singing

Charles Halsted attended Stanford University (BA, 1958), majoring in philosophy and European history. He graduated from the University of Rochester School of Medicine (MD, 1962) and obtained postgraduate medical training at the Cleveland Metropolitan General Hospital (1962-66). While serving as a US Public Health Service researcher in Cairo, Egypt (1966-68), he witnessed the Arab-Israeli war of June 1967. He then relocated to Baltimore, where he was a gastroenterology fellow at Johns Hopkins Hospital (1968-70) and an academic physician at Baltimore City Hospital. He joined the faculty at the University of California, Davis, School of Medicine in 1974 and retired in 2016. In addition to patient care and teaching, he carried out biomedical research that resulted in 105 original publications in peer-reviewed journals. During his ten-year tenure as editor of the *American Journal of Clinical Nutrition*, it became the leading international journal in its field. He prepared for a new career in poetry by taking online courses from Stanford Continuing Studies and by attending poetry workshops. In keeping with his past career, several of his poems explore human illness and relationships between physicians and patients.

CPSIA information can be obtained
at www.ICGtesting.com
Printed in the USA
LVHW011217021218
598978LV00012B/48/P

9 781635 347883